Photography Editor: RICHARD MAACK
Book Designer: MARY WINKELMAN VELGOS
Copy Editor: PK PERKIN McMAHON
Book Editor: BOB ALBANO
Map: GUS WALKER
Text for pages 26-27, 42-43, 50-51, and 60-61:
ARIZONA HIGHWAYS STAFF
Intern: EMILY LYONS

Library of Congress Control Number 2004112224
ISBN 1-932082-42-5
First printing, 2005. Second printing, 2006. Printed in Singapore.

Published by the Book Division of *Arizona Highways*® magazine, a monthly publication of the Arizona Department of Transportation, 2039 West Lewis Avenue, Phoenix, Arizona 85009.
Telephone: (602) 712-2200
Web site: www.arizonahighways.com

Publisher: WIN HOLDEN
Managing Editor: BOB ALBANO
Associate Editor: EVELYN HOWELL
Director of Photography: PETER ENSENBERGER
Production Director: KIM ENSENBERGER
Production Assistant: ANNETTE PHARES

ARIZONA HIGHWAYS
BOOKS

PREVIOUS PAGE: Cristy Yazzie is among the young people who foster the Navajo culture by wearing traditional attire. Her dress stands out especially well in the stark, rocky terrain.

NavajoLand

A Native Son Shares His Legacy

Text and Photographs by LeRoy DeJolie
With a Foreword by Tony Hillerman

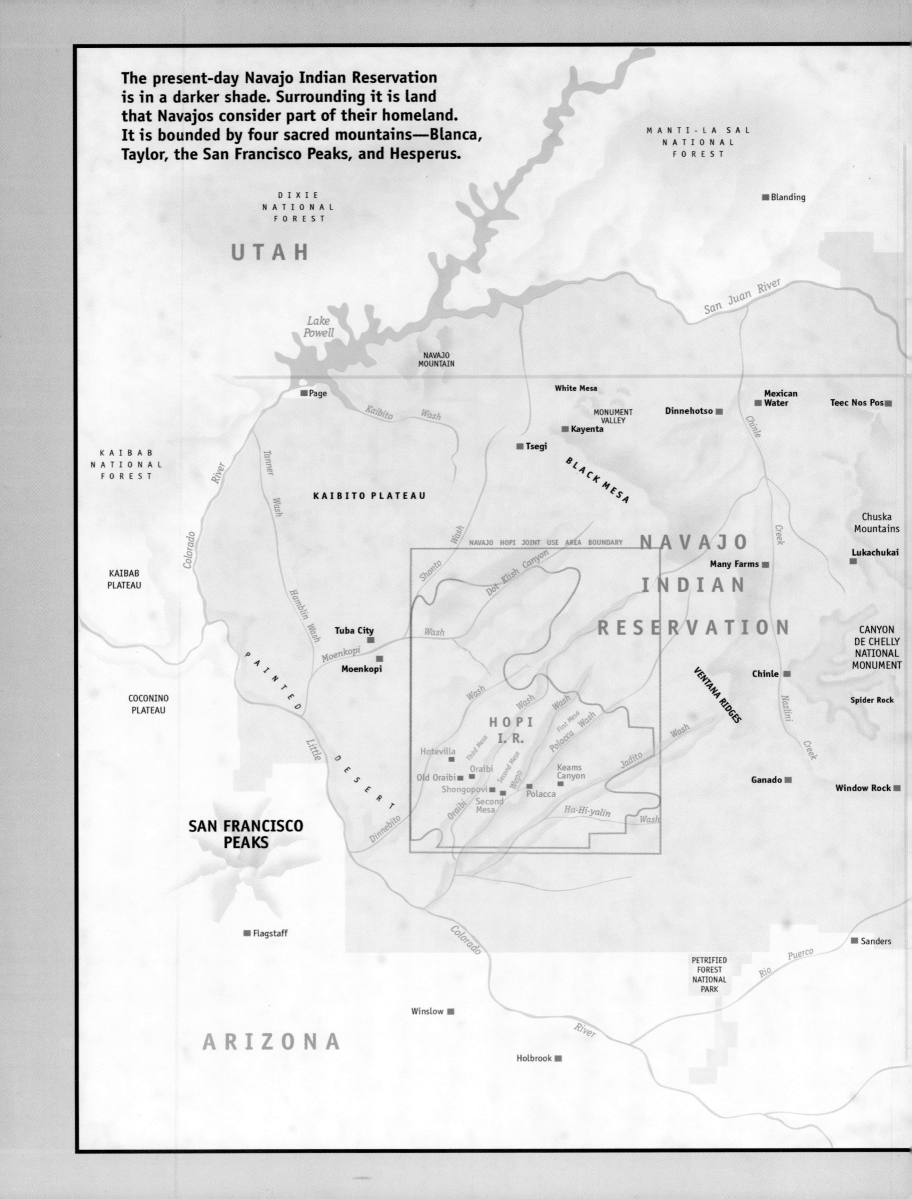

The present-day Navajo Indian Reservation is in a darker shade. Surrounding it is land that Navajos consider part of their homeland. It is bounded by four sacred mountains—Blanca, Taylor, the San Francisco Peaks, and Hesperus.

MANTI-LA SAL NATIONAL FOREST

DIXIE NATIONAL FOREST

■ Blanding

UTAH

San Juan River

Lake Powell

NAVAJO MOUNTAIN

■ Page

White Mesa

Mexican Water ■

Teec Nos Pos

MONUMENT VALLEY

Dinnehotso ■

Chinle Creek

Kaibito Wash

KAIBAB NATIONAL FOREST

Tanner Wash

■ Kayenta

■ Tsegi

BLACK MESA

Chuska Mountains

KAIBITO PLATEAU

Colorado River

Wash

NAVAJO

■ Lukachukai

KAIBAB PLATEAU

Hamblin Wash

NAVAJO HOPI JOINT USE AREA BOUNDARY

Shonto Wash

Dot-Klish Canyon

Many Farms ■

INDIAN

Tuba City ■

Wash

RESERVATION

CANYON DE CHELLY NATIONAL MONUMENT

Moenkopi Wash

■ Moenkopi

COCONINO PLATEAU

P A I N T E D

Wash

VENTANA RIDGES

Chinle ■

Nazlini Creek

Spider Rock

Little

D E S E R T

Wash

Wash

HOPI I. R.

Wash

First Mesa

Polacca Wash

Jadito Wash

Wash

Hotevilla ■

Third Mesa

SAN FRANCISCO PEAKS

Oraibi ■

Second Mesa

Wepo

Keams Canyon ■

Old Oraibi ■

Ganado ■

Shongopovi ■

Polacca ■

Window Rock ■

Dinnebito

Oraibi

Second Mesa

Ha-Hi-yalin

Wash

■ Flagstaff

Colorado

■ Sanders

PETRIFIED FOREST NATIONAL PARK

Rio Puerco

Winslow ■

River

A R I Z O N A

Holbrook ■

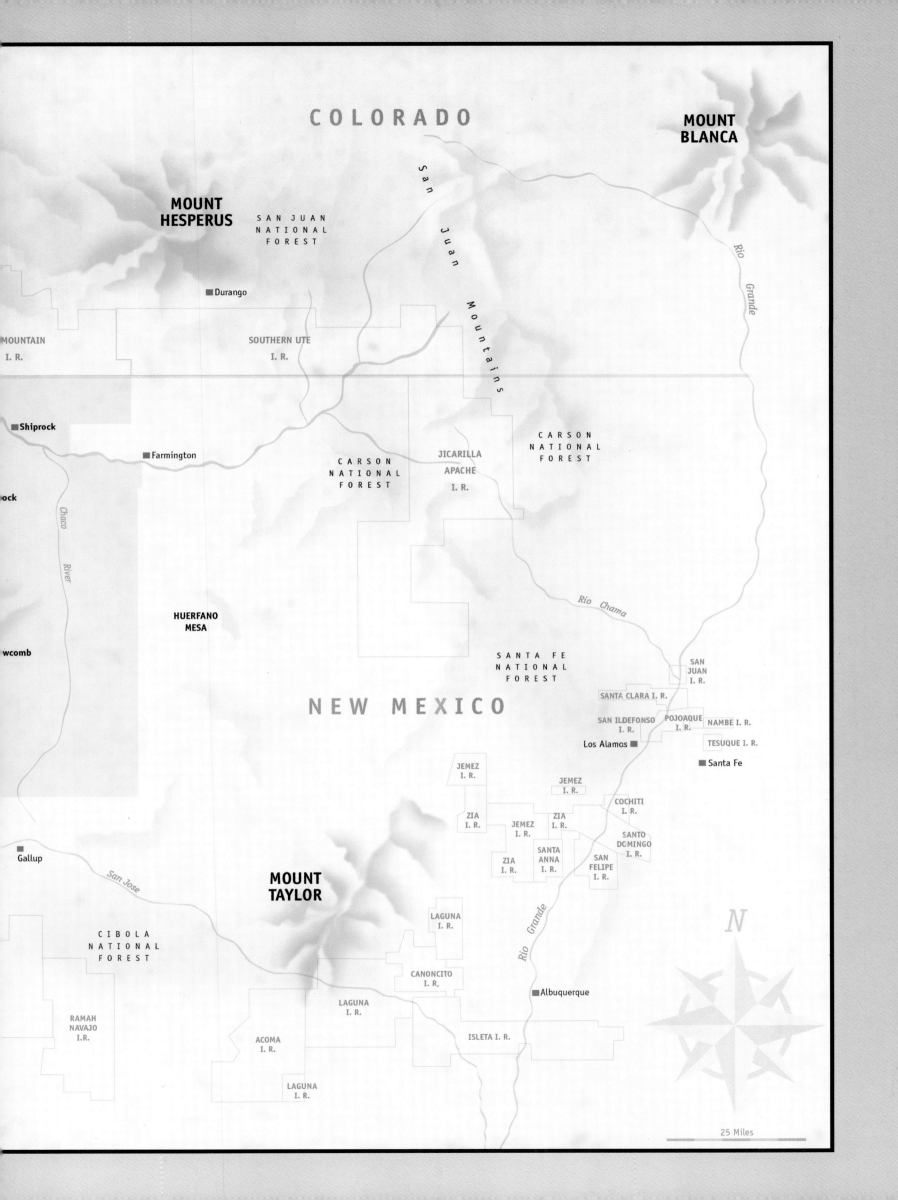

DEDICATION

To my daughters, Mariah Lynn and Tara Lyn DeJolie, two unique persons whose gentle, kind, and loving ways have given me a clearer vision of life's essentials for the last 17 years. They are the central inspiration of my photographic work. I thank them both most warmly for their unqualified patience and advice during the many months it took to compile these photographs and finish this book.

ACKNOWLEDGEMENTS

Primary credit goes to my parents, Harry and Florence. My motivation to take up photography derives from the countless hours of my youth spent with them. Also to the special friends and supporters I have had over the years: Thank you for your continual support and encouragement. My deep gratitude goes to Roxanne Vise for generous and unselfish assistance and for her many useful ideas in the genesis of this work. In addition, I am grateful to Robert and Brenda Sassman, who forever will be close friends. I also greatly appreciate the brilliant suggestions of Allan Csiky and his wife, Julie, and the technical support of Martha Vermeire. Finally, my heartfelt appreciation is given to the many anonymous individuals whom I have no way to thank personally — the men, women, and children shown in these pages. They represent Navajo life. Thanks a million.

EDITOR'S NOTE

A few explanations may help readers understand why some Navajo-word spellings in this book vary from those in other publications.

The basic reason is that Navajos primarily employed the oral tradition until well into the 20th century. Even today, some Navajos cling to word of mouth to pass along their language and accounts of their origin, history, and way of life.

In committing a language to written form, translators use an alphabet and diacritical marks to represent the sounds of each word. In the Navajo tongue, some words begin with a burst of sound, while others end abruptly; some letters require a high tone, or a drawn-out one; others feature a tone made by expelling air through the nose as a letter is uttered; other letters tell the speaker to tighten vocal cords, creating a glottal stop.

Thus, a word's spelling varies with the choices a translator makes to represent sounds, and on what he hears.

Likewise, although it is warm and personal, the oral tradition used over centuries allows story details to vary. So, foreword writer Tony Hillerman talks about "Born for Water," while author-photographer LeRoy DeJolie refers to this son of Changing Woman as "Sired by Water." They're the same deity.

Contents

9
[FOREWORD]
FOCUSING ON THE TRADITIONAL WAY

16
SHARING THE LEGACY OF DINÉ AND DINÉTAH

25
THE BEAUTY WAY

26
MOUNT BLANCA
[SACRED MOUNTAIN OF THE EAST]

42
MOUNT TAYLOR
[SACRED MOUNTAIN OF THE SOUTH]

50
SAN FRANCISCO PEAKS
[SACRED MOUNTAIN OF THE WEST]

66
MOUNT HESPERUS
[SACRED MOUNTAIN OF THE NORTH]

79
PHOTOGRAPHING NAVAJOLAND

80
INDEX

Extending from Page, Arizona, into Utah, Lake Powell forms a part of the northern edge of the Navajo Indian Reservation, but four sacred mountains bound *Dinétah* — the traditional homeland of the Navajo people that extends beyond reservation boundaries.

FOREWORD: FOCUSING ON THE TRADITIONAL WAY

BY TONY HILLERMAN

As far back as I can remember, *Arizona Highways* has used the work of great photographers to make the world aware of the beauty and variety of America's high desert country. That tradition continues in this book, but here it takes another step. It lets us see *Dinétah* (Din NAY Tah) — the land between the four sacred mountains (see map on pages 4-5) that mark the boundaries of Navajoland — through the eyes, camera lens, and culture of a Navajo artist steeped in the traditional ways of his people.

Some might ask why a cameraman born to the *Diné* (Din NAY) — the name traditional Navajos call themselves — would see this landscape in a way different from any other talented photographer. The answer lies in cultural values. LeRoy DeJolie was born to the Rock Gap People, his mother's clan, and the Red House People of his father. The photographer was raised among people who see more than mere mountains, dry washes, expanses of sage, and the solidified lava flow of exhausted volcanoes when they look at the landscape around them. DeJolie has heard the "winter stories" in which children of traditional Navajos learn lessons of their genesis from the start of creation.

For example, when a traditional Navajo focuses his camera on the old volcano we call Mount Taylor, he sees *Tsoodzil*, the Turquoise Mountain. The story of the Navajo Genesis tells how First Man formed the mountain of material brought up from the world below, decorated it with blue beads, pinned it to the Earth with a flint knife, and made it the home of the spirits Turquoise Boy and Yellow Corn Girl (the *Yei'* or Holy People known as *'Ashkii Dootl'izhii* and *'At'ééd Litso naadą́ą́*). On this mountain, the sacred southern boundary post of the Navajo Holy Land, the twin sons of Changing Woman — armed with weapons stolen from Sun — killed the *Ye'iitsoh*, the chief of the evil monsters who had followed the *Diné* up from the underworld. The lava flow, which forms the remarkable landscape we drive through south of Mount Taylor, consists of the dried blood of that monster. To traditional Navajos, the mountain remains an enduring reminder of how a harmonious family partnership allowed good to overcome greedy evil.

From the "winter stories" based on oral accounts from tribal mythology, traditional Navajo children learn their goal in life is not to be richer or more powerful than one's fellows. To the contrary, life's purpose is to remain in harmony with the great, interconnected cosmos of which they are a part — along with fellow humans, the birds, the wolves, the rivers, the hornets, the winter winds, the piñon trees and the bark beetles that feed on them, and even the mesa cliffs that change sunset colors with the changing seasons.

They are not (as the Bible's Book of Genesis suggests) born to be master of the planet and all upon it. Instead, Navajo children learn they are among the cogs

Wind, water, and other natural forces created this formation of spires in Monument Valley in a geologic process that began 25 million years ago. To the *Diné*, the spires rising from the common base constitute the Yei Bichei. The formation derives its name from Yeibichai, the Grandfather of the Spirits. The spire at left is the totem pole.

in an endless natural process, which includes not just us humans and not just all living things like the grass underfoot and the red-tailed hawk above, but also Earth itself, the starry sky, the clouds that drift through it, and the blessed rain they bring.

So, the Navajo photographer focuses on a holy land. My biblical atlas shows the crags of Mount Sinai as a tortured shape of eroded stones. Those of us raised in the Western traditions see Moses there, climbing down and carrying the Ten Commandments burned into a tablet of stone. In contrast, when we drive beside that long, narrow butte east of New Mexico Route 44 south of Bloomfield, we notice the radio towers lining its flat top. But the Navajo who is learned in the Navajo Genesis looks at that flat surface — Huerfano Mesa — and sees the place where First Man and First Woman heard the cries of an infant, carried her down, and brought her into womanhood with the first *Kinąąlda*, or puberty, ceremony. Thus was produced Changing Woman, who, like Moses, was to be the bringer of social laws.

The most important of all the Navajo Holy People, Changing Woman became the mother of the Hero Twins (Monster Slayer and Born for Water) and the great teacher of the people. The detailed instructions of this great *Yei'*, who in Navajo philosophy symbolizes Earth itself, range from exactly how a hogan should be built to many of the great healing ceremonies that keep individuals in harmony with each other and the world around them.

Directly to the point of this book, before Changing Woman disappeared in the west to join Sun, she left behind places that in the minds of traditional Navajos provoke memories of the lessons she taught. This crag beside old Highway 666 south of Shiprock is where Born for Water persuaded his brother not to kill Hunger Monster, because, without hunger, food would not be enjoyed. *K'idzííbáhí*, Grey Streak Mountain in the Tunicha Range above Lukachukai, is where the Holy People, or spirits, lived before humans evolved. That salmon-colored mesa cliff east of Gallup is where the *Yei'* Spider Woman (some call her Spider Grandmother) taught the Hero Twins how to reach Sun. And Chuska Peak (*Ch'óoshgai*) represents the head of *Yo'dí Dził* (Goods of Value Mountain) and is the source of key elements needed for the Night Chant curing ceremony. (In 1935, Navajo clan leaders and medicine men prevented Chuska's despoilment by blocking a United States Forest Service plan to build a lookout tower atop the mountain.

The Shiprock spire abounds in stories found in various versions of the Navajo Genesis. One suggests the old volcano core was a gigantic bird that carried the first of the *Diné* from the north, following the trail in the night sky formed by stars of the Milky Way. The most famous one tells how Monster Slayer climbed the spire, killed Winged Monster — which had preyed on the people — and gave the fledglings in Monster's nest the choice between being killed or converting themselves to less lethal birds. Thus were created the hawks and the owls.

Being a Navajo story, it must teach the need for social cooperation as well as tolerance. So when Monster Slayer finds himself with no way down from the spire, Spider Woman comes and rescues him with her weaving.

The Navajos were occupying the land bordered by their sacred mountains before Columbus discovered America, but it wasn't until 1868 that the U.S. government formally gave them title to part of it. That date was in the final chapter of the sad story remembered as the "Long Walk." Rumors of gold in the southern

Rockies had touched off a sudden interest in *Dinétah*. Navajos stood in the path of progress. Gen. James H. Carleton, military governor of the territory, issued his notorious General Order 15, ordering the subjugation of the tribe. U.S. Cavalry and militiamen swept through *Dinétah* to carry out his "scorched-earth" policy. They burned hogans, chopped down orchards, slaughtered sheep and cattle herds, and killed tribesmen who resisted. In the winter of 1864, more than 9,000 Navajos were herded into an internment camp at Bosque Redondo in eastern New Mexico. Families that escaped this roundup scattered into hiding places in the mountains.

By the next year, word of the inhumane conditions at Bosque Redondo began spreading. The Navajo prisoners had cleared 6,000 acres for farming and dug irrigation ditches to feed Pecos River water into their fields, but despite their labors, the land outside their sacred mountains remained hostile to them. The first year, cut worms destroyed most of their corn crop; in the second year, drought joined the worms to produce another failure. Alkali from the Pecos water was poisoning their fields. Firewood supplies were now exhausted, and mesquite root used for fuel was being carried in from miles away. A few escaped the camp, but Carleton's guards had orders to shoot any Navajo who went outside the fences.

Protests of these conditions rankled Congress. An investigation was ordered. Carleton was replaced. President Andrew Jackson assigned Gen. William Tecumseh Sherman to head a peace commission to solve the problem. Clan leaders were taken by train to the Arkansas River valley on the Oklahoma-Arkansas border for an inspection tour of the fertile, well-watered, game-rich land it offered. Then the captive Navajos were given three choices. They could move to a reservation in that fertile area. They could remain as farmers at Bosque Redondo. Or they could return to an area of about 3.4 million acres inside their sacred mountains.

The Book of Psalms in my Bible includes these lines —

Beside the streams of Babylon we sat

and wept at the memory of Zion

Jerusalem, if I forget you,

may my right arm wither . . .

— expressing the longing of the Jewish people held in Babylonian captivity. The minutes of the Proceedings of the Peace Commission, May 28, 1868, tell us what Barboncito, the man chosen by the tribe as spokesman, said when Sherman asked the Navajos for their thoughts. Barboncito made these points:

"The bringing of us here has caused a great decrease of our numbers. Many of us have died, also a great number of our animals. Our grandfathers had no idea of living in any other country except our own and I do not think it right for us to do so as we were never taught to. . . .

"This ground we were brought on, it is not productive. We plant but it does not yield; all the stock we brought here have nearly all died. . . . It is true we put seed in the ground, but it would not grow two feet high, the reason I cannot tell, only I think this ground was never intended for us. We know how to irrigate and farm, still we cannot raise a crop here . . . . [M]y mouth is dry and my head hangs in sorrow to see those around me who were at one time well off so poor now . . . . It seems that whatever we do here causes death . . . .

"I am speaking to you [General Sherman] now as if I was speaking to a spirit, and I wish you to tell me when you are going to take us to our own country."

Sherman granted the wish four days later. On June 1, 1868, a treaty returning *Dinétah* to the Navajos was signed by 16 Navajo leaders and by U.S. government officials. The "more than nine thousand" had been reduced to "about seven thousand" by conditions in Bosque Redondo. The Army provided some wagons to help them make the long trip across New Mexico. A few still had horses. Most walked.

Alex Etcitty remembered tales of that long walk. "When they topped the ridge at the Rio Grande and saw the Turquoise Mountain blue against the sunset "even the old warriors had tears of joy running down their faces."

Barboncito said this: ". . . Our country will brighten and the Navajos will be as happy as their land. Black Clouds will rise and there will be plenty of rain. Corn will grow in abundance and everything will look happy."

A few days earlier, when he was making his appeal for the return, the commission report quotes him like this:

"Now I am just like a woman, sorry like a woman in trouble. I want to go and see my own country."

In the chant of one of the great Navajo curing ceremonies, the singer has the *Yei'bichei*, (the talking god who speaks for the Holy People) saying this to the returning *Diné*:

This is your home, my grandchild,

he says to me as he sits down beside me.

My grandchild, I have returned you to your home

he says to me as he sits down beside me.

Upon the pollen figure I have returned

to sit with you, my grandchild.

Your home is yours again

Your fire is yours again

Your food is yours again

Your mountains are yours again, my grandchild.

He says as he sits beside me.

General Sherman told the President he doubted the Navajos could survive on that arid patch of desert, but — since it was utterly worthless by white standards — the whites would leave them alone. Sherman declared the reservation "as far from our future wants as it is possible to determine." Barboncito and the Navajos saw that landscape with a different set of eyes and a different set of values.

Which brings us to why it was wise to look at this bit of America through the eyes of a Navajo photographer. When Barboncito, the clan leader picked as spokesman, told Sherman the tribe had voted unanimously to return to *Dinétah*, he offered this explanation: "When the Navajos were created, four mountains and four rivers were pointed out to us. That was to be our *Dinétah*, and it was given to us by Changing Woman. . . . This woman gave us *Dinétah*, created it specially for us."

The yen for home is a common human trait. However, the choice so emphatically made by those Navajo hostages was between a fat and easy life in the fertile Arkansas River country and the hard times that would be wrought by returning to the high desert. Their choice is easier to understand when you consider the values taught in the Navajos' Book of Genesis.

For example: When the Third World of the *Diné* was destroyed by flood provoked by greed and selfishness, First Man emerged into this present world and discovered he had left his medicine bundle behind. It contained the elements he needed to cause evil, to cause hatred, anger, malice, and discontent. He summoned a heron, and asked this bird to dive back into the flood water and search for the bundle. He summed up all the "bad medicine" it contained by telling the heron it would be looking for "the way to make money."

A Navajo student in a class I taught years ago told me that if I wanted to find witchcraft on the reservation, "Look for a Navajo who has more of everything than he needs." Another Navajo friend told me that saying " 'rich Navajo' is like saying 'healthy corpse.' "

Alex Etcitty, my favorite *Diné* philosopher, explained that "having what you need is good. Having more than you need, with needy people around you, is a sign you're an evil person."

"Why evil?" I asked Etcitty.

"Because this sort of greed disrupts *hozhó*. And *hozhó* — a concept which includes not just harmony but contentment and family love — is the ultimate goal."

Thus, a traditional Navajo does not want to appear richer, or otherwise superior, to his neighbors. Instead of appearing wiser than others, he will precede an explanation with "They say," thereby giving the impression that he simply is passing along the knowledge. Or, for another example, a Navajo friend explained that his brother, who had won three consecutive rodeo bull-riding prizes at the Navajo Tribal Fair, would not enter the next year "because he has been winning too much."

In an interesting way, this different set of values seems to me reflected in attitudes toward beauty. As a farm boy, I was conditioned to see beauty in green alfalfa fields and endless rows of tall corn and to see failure in infertile places.

I never forget the day when Austin Sam and I were driving north up Arizona Route 191 toward Chinle. We passed the place where the slopes of Rock Mesa drain into *Bis'ii Ah* Wash and create a dramatic expanse of eroded wasteland stained red, blue, gray, and almost black by the variety of chemicals in the soil. It was spectacular under the morning sun, and the only color lacking was the green of growing things — the color that means money to agrarian people. I told Hosteen *(Hastíín)* [a Navajo term of respect] Sam that the old U.S. Geological Survey I had at home listed this place as "Desolations Flats."

"We call it Beautiful Valley," Sam said.

Happily, this book lets us see *Dinétah* through the camera lens of one of Hosteen Sam's fellow Navajos.

— *Tony Hillerman*
Albuquerque, New Mexico

16

SHARING THE LEGACY OF DINÉ AND DINÉTAH

PREVIOUS SPREAD:
Filling most of the
image with a rippled
sand foreground,
DeJolie bolsters its
apparent size so it's
not overpowered
by the rocky ridge
punctuated with
spires. The scene
calls to mind the
traditional Navajo
belief that harmony
and balance are
essential ingredients
of the environment
and life.
ABOVE: Elders such
as this grandmother
strive to give children
a context for life and
to instill the Navajo
culture in them.

Most people define time as consisting of years, months, days, hours, and
minutes. Ancient Hebrews and Chinese developed calendars and other
devices to keep track of time. Later, European civilization developed the
timekeeping methods we follow today to track time down to the millisecond.
Time puts us where we're supposed to be when we're supposed to be there. For
mainstream society, time and place are knotted firmly. When we think of events
in our past, we relate them to how old we were or when we experienced them. We
remember what we were doing when epic events occurred — the assassination of
President Kennedy or the explosion of the space shuttle Challenger.

To my people — we call ourselves *Diné*, the Navajo word for "the People"
— time remains more abstract than the years, hours, and minutes measured by
calendars and clocks. Yes, I wear a watch and show up when I'm expected in one
world. However, in my Navajo world, my concerns are more about culture, tradition,
relationships, and spirit. In this context, time is not a strict numerical concept as
much as it is an indicator of when people should plant or harvest, or when sheep
will breed or give birth.

So I won't dwell on time with historical dates and chronology.

Instead, I'll share stories told me by elders about how Navajo people came to be in *Dinetah*, the place that is our traditional homeland near what's known in North American geography as the Four Corners region, where Arizona, Utah, Colorado, and New Mexico meet. I'll tell about the traditions and beliefs that shape our view of the world, our sacred places, and our connection to the awesome landscape of our homeland. With that background (bear in mind that a story passed down over the centuries in the oral tradition can vary somewhat in details), I'll present photographs and explain how Navajo culture influences my passion for putting the spirit of Navajoland into photographic images. Thus, photographs in this book are not limited to the geographic boundaries of the Navajo Reservation. Some also record images and places long held by the Navajo people as their homeland, or *Dinétah*, the land bordered by four sacred mountains.

My own appreciation for the land began as a young Navajo shepherd, away from the noise and grime and traffic jams of cities. Though I attended schools in the distant cities of Phoenix and Los Angeles, my heart remained anchored to the red-rock canyons, mesas, and sage-covered rangeland of the Kaibito Plateau, the plateau just south of Navajo Mountain, in the farthest reaches of northern Arizona.

Away at school, my heart longed for the tranquil peace and beauty of my homeland. The sweet incense of cedar crackling in the fire, mixed with the aroma of brewing coffee in the morning, increased my longing for the dirt-floor hogan that I loved so much. I could never forget how, even on the coldest days, a bright, warm shaft of sunlight from the cobalt skies penetrated the hogan's smoke hole above, striking the inner gallery near the door, facing East, as Navajo culture dictates. The light illuminated everything, making it seem as though the interlocking cedar logs, which made up our traditional eight-sided structure, literally glowed with warmth.

The people, my relatives, gave context and texture to those striking scenes. Gathering with family and friends for festivals or ceremonies is an important aspect of Navajo life. My memories of those events are vivid. Everyone dressed in his or her best traditional attire. The brightly colored fabric, which contrasted with beautiful silver and turquoise jewelry, struck a visual impression that thrills me to this day. Then, there were the traditional foods: blue corn and pudding, fry bread, pinto beans and chili. These seemed to go perfectly with coffee that had been boiled down in an old pot on the fire. Of course, no gathering was complete without a freshly butchered lamb. The aroma of fresh mutton — roasting in cedar coals, or simmering in large pots of stew with hominy, potatoes, and corn — permeated the air.

There is boundless drama in *Dinétah* and in the Navajo culture. I am compelled to capture and preserve it in words underscored by photographic images for my family, for my people, and for generations to come. Among Navajos, the tradition of sharing stories has been a valuable tool to keep our ways and traditions alive throughout the centuries.

THE JOURNEY OF THE NAVAJO

Here in the rural setting of the Four Corners region, visitors will best savor the remarkable coziness and peculiar pace of ordinary Navajo life.

The story of the Navajo people has no beginning date. Navajo ritual singers (*Hataałii*) cannot convey whether the events they describe in their ancient songs occurred a hundred or a thousand years ago. Our songs, stories, and legends were simply compiled and preserved by oral tradition throughout the years.

The Navajo story, like those of many other people, begins with primitive, wandering people — the nomadic hunter-gatherers — who moved about on foot, living on wild vegetation — roots and berries — and hunting what animals they could find for meat.

Language helps map the Navajo journey. The only other Indians in the American Southwest with a language similar to the Navajos' are the Apaches. (There is a theory that our two tribes once were one people.) Except for Apache, no language like Navajo exists within at least a thousand miles of *Dinétah*. Yet, if a Navajo travels to Canada's British Columbia or Northwest Territories, he would hear familiar speech patterns and sounds and even would recognize some words. This language family is called the Athabaskan (*Diné nááhódló*).

Today, in various localities in British Columbia and the Pacific Northwest, natives who speak the Athabaskan language refer to themselves as *Diné*. We Navajos living in the Four Corners region can assume our forebears left their language in their wake as they journeyed to the land we now think of as ancestral, the land bordered by four sacred mountains in the Four Corners region.

The face of Curtie E. Daw reflects contentment, a trait especially valued by Navajos.

In their migration southward from the mountains of the Pacific Northwest, most of the Athabaskans stayed inland, among the deep forests of Alaska and British Columbia, where large animals, such as elk and deer, and fur-bearing animals were abundant. To their hunting skills the Athabaskans added trapping and fishing. They probably lived in log houses covered with earth. They wore simple clothes made of fur and moccasins made from animal skin. Today in British Columbia you can find remnants of the Athabaskan-speaking Sekani, who built log houses in upward-pointing shapes covered with bark and earth, much like the hogans built by Navajos over the last two centuries.

The broad migration from northern Athabaskan country included some people who traveled eastward and learned to hunt buffalo on the grassy plains, and others who moved into Oregon, where they became known as Sarsi. In California, they became known as the Karok and the Hupa.

Few clues of Athabaskan existence remain over the stretch of land that is now Nevada, Utah, and Colorado. However, quite surprisingly, ruins structured in the circumferential patterns of a hogan remain in the northwestern reaches of New Mexico, in the vicinity of Huerfano Mesa south of Bloomfield. In this region, Western anthropologists believe they have found the area where the Navajo people took root and developed the culture and traditions we follow today. From there our ancestors migrated westward.

WE ARE THE DINÉ — THE PEOPLE

We call ourselves the *Diné*. The name "Navajo" was given to us by other Indian tribes and by the white people. We have always been a people who adapt to survive. From our migrating ancestors' days, time and time again we have come across new ways of living and have made them our own. Farming, stock raising, silversmithing, and weaving, all of these skills we learned because we found them useful.

Navajo mythology tells us that Spider Man taught our ancestors how to make a loom and Spider Woman taught them how to weave. To this day, traditional Navajo weavers recognize that legacy with a "spirit line" woven into patterns. Documents written in the early 1700s by Spanish explorers in what's now the American Southwest mention the Navajos' weaving skills. By then, Navajo textiles were an important trade item.

The art of silversmithing was introduced to us by the Spaniards around the middle of the 19th century. Now, anyone interested in Indian silver thinks first of the Navajos. The *Diné* are highly skilled in their ability to create exquisite and multifaceted art in the form of jewelry. Gemstones, particularly turquoise, are inlaid to enhance the ornamental look. Navajo lore teaches that turquoise was brought to the present world by Holy People, so turquoise is especially valued because of its ceremonial significance.

We have always clung to the familiar — our livestock and ancestral land and stories of our history and culture. Many Navajos today continue the practice of sharing stories and singing the songs of our forefathers. Details of stories told in one clan may differ from details of the same story told in another clan. But essentially the stories explain who we have been and who we are. This is how we keep our ways and traditions alive for our children to follow. The high point of any culture is reached when the younger generation places high value on learning it. It thrills me when Navajos and non-Navajos come to know the sacred associations of *Diné* and *Dinétah*. However, I'm concerned that our culture is vanishing from the lives and memories of many of our people as they are swept into more dominant cultures around us and adopt new behavior — much as our ancestors did — to survive.

Our stories are told by the elders only in the wintertime when the snakes are asleep. Navajos, like other Indians, feel that serpents are the guardians of sacred lore and will punish those who treat it lightly. Our stories are full of poetry and

A youngster embracing Navajo culture prompts DeJolie to call her interest a high point for older members of the tribe who follow traditional ways.

accounts of epic events. One of the events is referred to as the Long Walk.

The tragic story began in 1863 when the U.S. Army under Col. Kit Carson uprooted 9,000 or more members of my tribe from their homes and hiding places. The soldiers laid waste to dwellings, stock animals, and stored foods, and they held the people captive. In the following year, the soldiers drove the Navajos — in a march line that extended for 8 miles — to Bosque Redondo in eastern New Mexico, where they were forced to help build the Army's Fort Sumner and live under wretched conditions for years.

During the period of exile, so strong was the call of the homeland that several hundred Navajos escaped and fled to the western regions among the slot canyons on the Colorado Plateau. There they joined those who had not been captured. Once a treaty was signed in 1868, the Army freed the remaining exiles, most of whom returned to *Dinétah*. By then, the Navajos had lost perhaps 25 percent of their people.

For the first years of life, a Navajo child is either strapped in a cradleboard or to his mother's back, sharing her warmth and rhythm in a half-drowsy state. Perhaps, it is this secure closeness to the mother's body that gives the Navajo his remarkable acceptance of fate and his usually wonderful recollection of childhood. Before he can form thoughts, the Navajo child experiences the daily rhythms of life, something I believe imbues us with a deep cultural bond that lies beneath our consciousness.

Beyond the immediate family, Navajo clanships form a single, vertical bond in social relationships between individuals and family groups, with all members sharing basic equality and basic commodities. As a result of the close ties of clanship, the household becomes stronger as our lineage forms a binding sense of solidarity.

Each Navajo clan is like an extended family whose clan members call each other Sister or Brother, Mother or Father, and Grandmother or Grandfather, even if they are not so related by blood. Since the members of each clan feel themselves descended from one woman, they count their relationships through maternal, not paternal, lineage. For example, Navajo girls born into the Red House Clan or the Bitter Water Clan can pass that particular clan onto their children. Navajo males born into the clan must marry girls from outside the clan — this is a strict requirement — and their children enter the clan of the mother.

My father is part of the *Kinł ichíi'nii* clan, known as the Red House People; my mother is a member of the *Tsé deeshgizhnii*, the Rock Gap People. Following tradition, my clan is that of my mother.

THE FOUR SACRED MOUNTAINS

Following the reality that nature in Navajoland is bountiful and beautiful, the *Diné* believe all that is beautiful also is good and pure. Similarly, we revere any element of Mother Earth and Father Sky (male and female are always represented) or any place that inspires us with awe and wonder.

There is a wild country described to me by storytellers as Old Navajoland, the place where our people originated. It's not located, however, on the present-day Navajo Reservation, but east of it, in the highlands below Mount Blanca, one of the four mountains that the Navajos hold sacred. The Navajo creation story tells us that

In Navajo mythology, horses were a gift from the Holy Spirits to help the people hunt. Today, horse riding remains a lifestyle choice for many Navajos.

the *Diné* passed through three worlds before emerging into the fourth world, our present place, known as Glittering World.

It is here in the region defined by Mount Blanca that the Earth people first arrived, climbing up from the underworld through a giant, magical reed. From out of this house of lights and rainbows came people with fur and feathers on their strange masks. They met to arrange the fourth world. In the worlds below, there always had been four mountains marking each of the four directions, and the Navajos named the directions in this order: East, South, West and North.

So, the Holy People brought along four sacred mountains and placed them to mark the four directions in the fourth world. The mountains are named Mount Blanca in the East, Mount Taylor in the South, San Francisco Peaks in the West, and Mount Hesperus in the North. Together, they tell us where our homeland is.

Mount Blanca, the eastern mountain in what now is Colorado, is made of white shell and is called *Sisnaajiní* in Navajo, translated as "the mountain with the dark streaks across it."

Mount Taylor in the south, made of exquisite turquoise, is called *Soodził* and is located near present-day Grants, New Mexico.

On the slopes in northern Arizona lie the San Francisco Peaks, an imposing formation punctuating the landscape near present-day Flagstaff. In Navajo, it is called *Dook'o'oosłííd*, meaning, "where the snow never melts." This mountain is made of abalone.

Last is the northern mountain, made of jet, Mount Hesperus, or *Dibé nitsaa* meaning "place of big sheep." It's located in the La Plata range in southwestern Colorado. The reservation occupies only a part of the territory bounded by these four mountains.

Not surprisingly, Navajo fancy dancers are distinguished by costume as well as choreography. Perhaps more. An Internet Web site forum devoted to "pow wows" — a social gathering of Indians — asked participants to name the best fancy dancer and explain their votes. Replies included: "He has creative footwork and wicked outfits; he is a total cutie; he's my cousin, thatz why; and, awesome dancing, awesome outfit."

Built perhaps two or three generations ago, this hogan in Canyon de Chelly likely served as a summer home for a Navajo family. The door faces eastward, toward the rising sun, as tradition dictates.

The newly arrived Holy People placed two travelers in the sky, carrying bright shields, which soon became the sun and the moon. They meant to place bright stars in an orderly arrangement, but a mischievous coyote scattered them and spoiled the plan.

The Holy People placed other mountains around the land. A mysterious bird constantly dove to the bottom of the great sea to gather jewels, perhaps suggesting the origin of the white abalone shell that formed the eastern mountains.

Navajo legends told to me speak of Pedernal Peak, where a magical baby girl was found, wrapped in glittering attire. She is spoken of as *'Asdzáán nádleehé,* or Changing Woman, also the name of a Navajo clan. Old Navajo songs that I've heard over the years claim that Changing Woman personifies the Earth, which changes every year from being green and grassy to brown and dry. The old songs point out steep-sided Huerfano Mesa, the place located just south of today's Bloomfield, New Mexico, where Changing Woman was raised. This area has become known as *Dziłná'oodiłii,* the corridor to present-day *Dinétah.* Changing Woman then married Sun and also Water, and she bore twin boys, one was Monster Slayer and the other Sired by Water. In four short years, the pair grew into manhood. They visited Sun, who gave them armor of flint and swords of straight and jagged lightning. With these weapons, the two young war gods traveled over Old Navajoland, slaying monsters.

The locations of these events and encounters are known, for often the bodies were turned to stone and can still be seen in the shape of rocks and pinnacles. Near Mount Taylor is *Yei'ii'tseh,* the place where a giant sucked people in. When the gods killed him, his blood flowed out in a stream, which is now black lava, backed up for 10 miles.

In the foothills of Carrizo Mountain and in the desert adjacent to Farmington,

New Mexico, lived the man-eating eagle, whose body is now stone with sharp feathers pointing upwards and with wings trailing on the ground. Today, we call this place Shiprock.

Chaco Canyon was the place of the bear who killed people then walked back on his own tracks so no one knew where he went. At Aztec was Kicking Off Rocks, who kicked people into the San Juan River. Near the present Taos Mountains was the monster Rocks That Rush Together, which crushed people. And on a cliff in Colorado were gigantic rock swallows, which clawed and pecked travelers to death. The twins disposed of every one of these with the help of Fly, Spider Woman, Bat Woman, and Gopher.

Finally, all of the monsters were gone with the exception of Old Age, Sickness, Poverty, and Death, which remain here to keep mankind alert and working. The birds and animals have retired to the woods, trees, and caves, dressed forever in their coats of fur and feathers, and the masked spirits, which chose their homes on the top of the mountains, remain there to this day.

Stories and places. Sometimes they're inseparable in my mind's eye. The traditional Navajo dwelling place is called a hogan. It's basically circular in shape and varies in size according to the needs of the family living in it. Typically, an old-style hogan is covered snugly with earth. For me, a hogan also recalls stories and traditions. Its doorway juts out eastward, meeting the rising sun, as did the doorway built for First Man and First Woman. Looking at Cabezon Peak in New Mexico, non-Navajos see a tall, pyramid-shaped rock standing alone in the desert. But according to some Navajo elders, this site is the Holy Hogan, turned to stone.

For me, looking at Navajoland through a camera adds depth to the meaning of both the stories and the places.

The Beauty Way

Mother earth, Father sky.

Our Father the Sun, our Mother the Moon.

Mount Blanca from the East here I come with beauty before me.

Mount Taylor from the South here I come with beauty before me.

San Francisco Peaks from the West here I come with beauty before me.

Mount Hesperus from the North here I come with beauty before me.

Bless me with the everlasting life.

The beautiful corn pollen road I will walk in beauty.

Beauty will lie ahead of me.

Beauty will lie behind me.

Beauty will lie above me.

Beauty will lie around me.

Corn Pollen Boy, Corn Pollen Girl, may there be beauty ahead of me.

There may be beauty.

There may be beauty.

There may be beauty.

There may be beauty.

A BEAUTY PRAYER STORY (As told by Sherafina "Dee Dee" Bob, Navajo entertainer):

We are known as Diné, which means the people.

Our Creator only knows where the beginning is.

We Diné people believe that the Creator had a thought to create light in the East.

The thought went to the South to create water.

The thought went to the West to create air.

The thought went to the North to create pollen from emptiness.

The thought went to the center, this pollen became earth.

The light, the air, the water, and the earth are contained within nature.

Our belief, that all natural world has an interconnection and equalness within us.

That is why our Beauty Prayer starts with our four holy directions.

Silhouettes, colors, and shadows spewing from a rising sun in Monument Valley, left, call to mind the Beauty Way Prayer, which often is recited just before dawn.

Mount Blanca

[SACRED MOUNTAIN OF THE EAST]

Sisnaajiní **MOUNTAIN WITH DARK STREAKS ACROSS IT.**

The Holy People, or spirits, taught the Diné to address their four sacred mountains and corresponding directions beginning in the East and progressing clockwise to the South, West, and North. These mountains define the boundaries of Dinétah, the land given to the Diné by Changing Woman.

In creating the current, Glittering World, the Holy People fastened Mount Blanca, white mountain, to Earth by a lightening bolt, decorating it with white shells, white lightning, white corn, and dark clouds, and covering it with a sheet of daylight. Then they brought small, stone images of Rock Crystal Boy and Rock Crystal Girl from the underworld and set them on the mountain, where they came alive.

Mount Blanca, as all the sacred mountains do, provides a prominent landmark by which traveling Navajos can determine their location and home. As one Diné legend holds, when a father taught his two young boys about worldly matters, both sweet (tobacco), and dark (war), he took them on many travels throughout Dinétah. At different points he would ask them, "Where do you belong in the world? Show me your home."

Sisnaajiní

As they walked along flat lands, the boys became confused. They could not say where they belonged, nor whether they were home. Only when they saw the mountains — each with a distinct personality represented by the colors white, turquoise, yellow, and black — could the boys could find their way and feel the rhythms of their homeland and their people.

The *Diné* believe there is a male and a female to all things. In the Navajo view, rain, one of Earth's four main elements (the others are light, air, and pollen) is designated as male when it falls in stormy sheets accompanied by lightning. In contrast, gentle, female rain soothes. Male downpours help distinguish Mount Blanca from the other sacred mountains.

Mount Blanca lies in the Sangre de Cristo range in southern Colorado's San Luis Valley near Alamosa. Within the range there are large populations of elk and Rocky Mountain bighorn sheep. Ten mountains in the range reach higher than 14,000 feet — Mount Blanca stands at 14,345 feet — with skiing and rock-climbing locations found throughout the range.

Following are images from the eastern part of *Dinétah*.

The interplay of sand dunes and hoodoos or goblins made of Navajo sandstone, left, creates
a dramatic scene at Ventana Ridges near Chinle. The ridges extend some 40 miles across the
Chinle Basin. To capture the image above, DeJolie slept overnight below Ventana Ridges to be
ready with his camera at first light. The view toward the window in the rock is northward. The
name Ventana is derived from a Spanish word meaning window.

An autumn storm leaves water below the north side of a ridge, above, at the mouth of Canyon de Chelly, creating a scene that exists only after a rain. A few hours later, on the ridge's south side, right, receding water fashions scallops in the sand.

Hoping to steer their children along what Navajos refer to as the "beauty way" of living in harmony and balance, some parents tell children that the white mass atop Spider Rock in Canyon de Chelly consists of bones of "bad children" left there by Spider Woman, who also taught the Navajos how to weave. On the horizon at top right lie the Lukachukai Mountains.

A wide-angle lens helps capture the extent of badlands sculpted from what geologists call the Chinle Formation, which generally consists of shale, silt, and fine- and coarsely-grained sandstone with volcanic ash. However, this scene is in what Navajos call Beautiful Valley at the southern end of Chinle Wash near Nazlini.

Spires of white gypsum create a formation calling to mind a cathedral. Named Salahkai (sometimes Balakai) Mesa, it is located in the Chinle Basin. One of the Navajo terms for the formation means "white sand," and it is associated with the Blessing Way tradition.

Viewed from its western side, above, and its eastern flank, opposite, Shiprock and the ridge extending some 3 miles from it form a prominent landmark in northwestern New Mexico. It was here that one of Changing Woman's twin sons, Sired by Water, persuaded his brother not to kill Hunger Monster, because hunger is necessary for people to enjoy food.

Clumps of rabbit brush adorn the banks of the Chaco River in New Mexico after it has flowed through what today is the Chaco Culture National Historical Park, the site of ancient Puebloan ruins.

Elsewhere along the Chaco River, near Blanca Trading Post, grass and reeds line the banks. The area is part of a corridor linking the Navajo point of emergence from the underworld to the rest of the land defined by four sacred mountains. In escaping from an underworld, ancestors of the Navajos crawled up a reed.

These formations near Newcomb, New Mexico, consist primarily of soft rock that allowed the elements to shape them into the appearance of elephant feet. The formations contain traces of coal, and the larger one at left has a hole bored by erosion.

A piece of nature's handiwork decorates a stark landscape near Newcomb, New Mexico. The layered rock easily breaks with light pressure.

MOUNT TAYLOR

[SACRED MOUNTAIN OF THE SOUTH]

Soodził' **TURQUOISE MOUNTAIN**

The *Diné* know Mount Taylor as the peak that is fastened to Glittering World by a great knife made of flint. Atop the mountain, the spirits placed a turquoise basket containing two bluebird eggs covered with sacred buckskin. Brilliant flecks of turquoise, dark mist, female rain, and various animals author the mountain's character and beauty.

When the *Diné* returned in 1868 from exile in Bosque Redondo, New Mexico, the first sight of a familiar landform caused them to fall to the ground and weep: It was Turquoise Mountain, which, in Navajo mythology, is home of the chief of the enemy gods and monsters. The *Diné* word for "monster" translates literally to "that which obstructs a successful life." The *Diné* believe that one way to decrease the power of an enemy, or monster, is to name it.

The mountain is important to the Blessing Way and Enemy Way ceremonies. The Blessing Way opens the door to Glittering World and is associated with a time when the *Diné* and Puebloan peoples interacted, while the Enemy Way rids a Navajo from evil imparted by an enemy. After World War II, Enemy Way ceremonies were

Soodził'

conducted for many of the famed Navajo Code Talkers who had fought in the war's Pacific Theater.

Located near Grants, New Mexico, midway between Albuquerque and Gallup, Mount Taylor lies in the southwestern part of the San Mateo Mountains. In Southwestern history, the mountain was once called San Mateo but was renamed after Zachary Taylor, an Army general who became well known during the Mexican War and later became president.

Mines in the Turquoise Mountain area have consistently produced high-grade turquoise for Navajo silversmiths.

For several decades, the Mount Taylor Ranger District in the Cibola National Forest has worked to restore and heal the area, which was severely affected by intense grazing, logging, and road-building. Lava flows lie to the south and northeast of the peak, and the peak is snow-capped until late spring. At 11,389 feet, Mount Taylor can be seen from a distance of a hundred miles.

Following are images from the southern part of *Dinétah*.

For LeRoy DeJolie, these hoodoos represent more than mounds sprouting from a sandy base. Before taking the picture near Cottonwood in eastern Arizona on the Navajo Reservation, he stood there alone for an hour as the scene nurtured in him a sense of reverence and awe.

In some Navajo stories, this area is considered to be the feet of Pollen Mountain, a huge female anthropomorphic figure consisting of several formations including Navajo Mountain and several buttes and mesas.

The ruins of this hogan call to mind the Blessing Way, a ceremony that includes an account of how the first hogan was built for First Man and First Woman with precise instructions. The structure probably was used for ceremonies. Joining forked-tip (female) and straight (male) logs symbolizes a strong partnership between a husband and wife.

Although the hogan on this homestead features a roof with modern material and a stove, the design follows the construction prescribed for a traditional Navajo home.

Runoff water gathers in a drainage below the silhouetted Black Mesa at sunset. When the U.S. Army invaded Navajoland in the mid-1860s, many Navajos hid in remote reaches of Black Mesa, which is considered to be the body of the female anthropomorphic figure known as Pollen Mountain (see Page 45).

San Francisco Peaks

[SACRED MOUNTAIN OF THE WEST]

Dook'o'oosłííd **WHERE THE SNOW NEVER MELTS**

The number four has sublime significance for the *Diné*. The rhythm of the four seasons is essential to life and nourishment. Many Navajo storytellers recount *Diné* journeys through four worlds: The first is symbolized by black, the second blue, the third yellow, and the fourth, or present world, is glittering. Navajo mythology, the details of which tend to vary from clan to clan, delineates four original clans: Towering House, One Walks Around You, Bitter Water, and Mud. And four mountains mark the four directions, providing the boundaries to the sacred land of the *Diné*.

Each sacred mountain is associated with one color, and the San Francisco Peaks take the color yellow. Known as Abalone Shell Mountain and "where the snow never melts," the Peaks' significance as a wellspring of spiritual belief extends beyond Navajo culture to include prominence in the belief systems of the Hopi, Hualapai, Zuni, Yavapai, and several Apache tribes.

The three principal peaks of the mountain complex — Humphreys (Arizona's highest summit at 12,655 feet), Agassiz (12,300 feet), and Frémont (11,940 feet)

Dook'o'oosłííd

— were born in a series of fierce volcanic eruptions over 2 million years ago and are part of the San Francisco volcanic field. Time has softened the peaks into the rolling, fluid shapes seen today.

Diversity is the prime feature of the San Francisco Peaks, which nurture ecosystems as dissimilar as alpine tundra and Sonoran desert and provide a home for more than 200 species of mammals and birds, among them elk, bear, wild turkey, candytuft, lupine, and the San Francisco Peaks groundsel, which grows nowhere else in the world.

The Peaks, named by Spanish missionaries for Saint Francis of Assisi, have many uses. Winter snow and late summer monsoon rain soak into the volcanic rock, supplying much of the water for the city of Flagstaff; skiers and hikers regularly enjoy their slopes and trails; and the Peaks have been used for grazing, logging, and mining — fueling controversy between conservationists and those who seek remuneration for tapping into the area's abundant natural resources.

Following are images from the western part of *Dinétah*.

Writing of his birthplace and the high country where he worked as a shepherd, LeRoy DeJolie says, ". . . my heart remained anchored to the red-rock canyons, mesas, and sage-covered rangeland of the Kaibito Plateau" in northern Arizona.

White Mesa Arch reigns over the southeastern end of the mesa in northern Arizona. It was in this area that many Navajos hid from soldiers before the Long Walk. Formed from Dakota sandstone, the arch spans 53 feet, rises 84 feet over its base, and has a thickness of 73 feet.

Alstrom Point reaches into Lake Powell near a site where, at about the time of the American Revolution, two Spanish explorer-priests — Dominguez and Escalante — found a crossing over the Colorado River. The scene at left looks northward over a bay to the Grand Staircase-Escalante National Monument on the horizon. The view eastward from the point, above, includes Navajo Mountair at sunrise.

The Colorado River cut into the Colorado Plateau to form Horseshoe Bend before Glen Canyon
Dam was built upriver at Page, Arizona. The river flows from right to left.

Carved buttes, gulches, and mounds are a part of the rugged landscape of
Glen Canyon not covered by Lake Powell.

Water Holes Canyon, above and right, cuts through Navajo sandstone, much of it cross-bedded, a few miles south of Page, Arizona. The canyon draws its name from numerous pockets in the sandstone that catch rain and runoff water.

A gathering storm intrudes on the midday sun over the Grand Canyon. The light bearing on the foreground makes the terrain seem flatter than it really is.

Viewed from a distance, the Vermilion Cliffs appear as a 40-mile long sheer-faced escarpment. Up close, their mass transforms into a myriad of rock formations.

Shafts of lights poking through dark clouds create patches of brilliance on the Echo Cliffs near Tuba City.

Imagine you're standing at the base of a tall, broad cliff. Look at the cliff's face and imagine a passageway burrowing into the cliff, top to bottom, in a meandering route. The walls of the passageway are sculpted into smooth swirls, protrusions, and recesses. That's a slot canyon, such as Lower Antelope Canyon, above and left. Slot canyons are formed by rushing water — the Navajo name for Upper Antelope Canyon means "where water runs through rocks."

66

MOUNT HESPERUS

[SACRED MOUNTAIN OF THE NORTH]

Dibé nitsaa **PLACE OF BIG MOUNTAIN SHEEP**

In a heavily wooded area of southern Colorado rich with streams, lakes, and rivers rises the mountain the *Diné* know to have been fastened to the sky with a rainbow and decorated with jet, dark mist, and wild animals. It is the Sacred Mountain of the North, known to Navajos variously as Jet Mountain, Coal Mountain, Obsidian Mountain, or "place of big mountain sheep." On the maps it is called Mount Hesperus or Hesperus Peak, a name which is taken from Longfellow's poem, "The Wreck of the Hesperus."

Traditional belief holds the mountain has been shrouded in a dark blanket and beaded with obsidian. Atop the peak lies an obsidian basket holding dark beads and two blackbird eggs, covered with buckskin. The resident gods, Pollen Boy and Grasshopper Girl, were formed from a great bundle of things gathered from the world below.

According to instructions given in the creation story, the placement of the posts of the traditional Navajo dwelling, the hogan, echo the positioning of the four sacred mountains. Navajos learn that the journey through life is a circular

Dibé nitsaa

one. Custom dictates that after entering a hogan one should progress through the home in a clockwise direction to show respect. Likewise, when enumerating the four sacred mountains, respect is shown by starting in the East and following a clockwise (positive) pattern, concluding with the Sacred Mountain of the North.

Mount Hesperus, which reaches 13,225 feet, is situated within the La Plata range of the San Juan Mountains. The mountains have been mined extensively for silver and gold, and they contain grasslands; wetlands; sub-alpine parks; forests of aspen, ponderosa pine, oak, and Douglas fir; and meadowlands, which provide habitats for sensitive species that have not been found anywhere else in the world. As the last known location of some arctic mosses and relics of the last ice age, they harbor six wilderness areas and the headwaters of the Rio Grande, San Juan, Dolores, and Animas rivers.

Following are images from the northern part of *Dinétah*.

Under the influence of light and shadows, Monument Valley, left and above, continually changes color. In Navajo mythology, the valley — which includes about 600 square miles of which about 100 square miles form a tribal park — is considered to be a huge hogan.

Towering about a thousand feet above the valley floor, the Mittens are among the most prominent landmarks in Monument Valley. In Navajo tradition, they are hands left by the spirits as a sign that they would return.

Geologic forces, wind, and rain began forming Monument Valley more than 20 million years ago after a sea receded, leaving an ocean of sand. Many of the formations represent deity figures for Navajos.

Hunt's Mesa lies in a remote area of Monument Valley, reachable by hiking or four-wheel-drive vehicle.

A century old piñon tree adds a dramatic touch to this view of Hunt's Mesa.

This place, above and right, is called Red Mesa, located less than 20 miles from the Four Corners, where Arizona, Utah, Colorado, and New Mexico meet. It's stark, but yellow mule's ears thrive in the sandy plains below the mesa top. Navajo mythology relates that the red in the rock came from one of Monster Slayer's conquests.

The final seconds of sunlight cast a bluish tint over a volcanic formation, above, known as El Capitan, Agathla Peak, or — in some Navajo stories — "much wool," a site where coarse rocks facilitated the scraping of hair from animal hides. The formation lies at the southern end of Monument Valley. The butte in the upper image is a volcanic plug near Kayenta and is named Church Rock. Some Navajo accounts suggest the formation once was a giant ant hill.

Photographing Navajoland

Soft, sweet light bathes the canyon walls and plateaus of my homeland on the Colorado Plateau in brilliant bands of dark rose, pink, and tan. Although I often feel dwarfed by the immense size and striking shapes of these timeless sentinels, I live for the opportunity to capture them on film.

I see my work more as a mission than a job. It is my lifetime ambition to help preserve the heritage our Navajo ancestors desired for succeeding generations — a heritage that intertwines with the land. For many of our people, that heritage is vanishing from their lives and memories as they are swept into the more dominant cultures around us.

Taking a documentary approach, I want my images to inform viewers about the landscapes I photograph. To infuse a personal sense of depth and perception into my photographs, I draw heavily on my experiences in Navajo culture as it relates to the landscapes. Besides the usual photographic elements of light, shape, and texture, my comprehension of the subject at hand is influenced by smell, sound, previous experiences, and the feelings of the moment. Thus, I like to compare images I create to the art of a Navajo silversmith refining silver and stones from a crude state into jewelry with inlaid turquoise, or to the drama of a weaver employing patterns, texture, color, and symmetry to form an intricately designed Navajo rug.

As a landscape photographer, I have to be ready to seize opportunities. I must have an eye for the changing light conditions and the ability to predict and wait for the "right" lighting. The exquisite beauty of sunrise and sunset in my homeland can seem to linger, but in a photographic sense, passes very quickly. I've learned to rise well before dawn or stay out late to take advantage of the "sweet light," which makes a scene appear almost timeless and limitless.

Photographers elsewhere capture the beauty of sunsets amid the floral and sensuous roundness of rolling green hills for a dramatic photograph. I create my images using that with which nature has blessed me. Here in Navajoland, from the purity of the windswept dunes to the subtle hues of massive hard ridges and sculpted, soft sandstone canyon walls, I feel very much a part of my homeland, and my homeland is very much part of me.

The cameras I primarily used for this book were a Wista DX II wooden-body field camera and a 1952 Deardorff, with a film holder reconstructed by Keith Canham of Mesa, Arizona, from an 8x10-inch to a 4x10 format for panoramic shots. These large-format cameras present unique opportunities for depth of field, sharpness, and image quality despite the limitations posed by lens diameters — 75mm, 90mm, 210mm, and 300mm with my 4x5 camera — and the limited flexibility of the bellows with my 8x10 camera.

I used a single lens reflex (SLR) camera for both people and close-up detail shots. My film was exclusively Fuji Velvia for landscape and Fuji Provia for my people and detail subjects.

INDEX

Agassiz Peak, 51
Agatha Peak, 78
Alaska, 18
Albuquerque, 43
Alstrom Point, 54-55
Anasazi, see Puebloan (ancient)
Animas River, 67
Antelope Canyon (Upper & Lower) 64-65
Apaches, 18, 50
Arkansas River, 12
Athabaskan, 18
Aztec, 23

Beautiful Valley, 13, 34
Bis'ii Ah Wash, 13
Blanca Trading Post, 39
Bob, Sherafina "Dee Dee," 25

Canada, 18
Canyon de Chelly, 22, 3C-31, 32-33, back cover
Cabezon Peak, 23
Carrizo Mountains, 22
ceremonies, 17
    Beauty Way, 25, 32
    Blessing Way, 35, 42, 46
    chant, 12
    Enemy Way, 42
    Kinaalda, 10
    Night Chant, 10
Chaco Canyon, 23
Chaco Culture NHP, 38
Chaco River, 38-39
Changing Woman, 10, 12, 22, 26, 36, 76
Chinle, 13, 29
Chinle Basin, 29, 35
Chinle Formation, 34
Church Rock, 78
Chuska Mountains, 38
Cibola National Forest, 43
clans
    Bitter Water, 20, 50
    Changing Woman, 22
    Mud, 50
    One Walks Around You, 50
    Red House, 9, 20
    Rock Gap, 9, 20
    Towering House, 50
Colorado Plateau, 20, 56
Colorado River, 55-56
Cottonwood (Navajo Reservation town) 35, 44
creation/origin story
    Bat Woman, 23
    bear, 23

Born for Water (Sired by Water) 10, 22, 36, 76
Changing Woman, 10, 12, 22, 26, 36, 76
Corn Pollen Boy, Girl, 25
Coyote, 22
Father Sky, 20
First Man, Woman, 9-10, 12, 23, 46
Fourth World, 21, 42, 50
Fly, 23
Glittering World, see Fourth World
Gopher, 23
Grasshopper Girl, 66
Hero Twins, 10, 22, 23
heron, 12
Holy People/Spirits (Yei') 10, 19, 20-23, 26, 70
Hunger Monster, 10, 36
Monster Slayer, 10, 22, 76
monsters, 23
Moon, 22
Mother Earth, 20
Pollen Boy, 66
Rock Crystal Boy, Girl, 26
rock swallows, 23
Spider Man, 19
Spider Woman, 10, 19, 23, 32
Sun, 10, 22, 76
Third World, 12
Turquoise Boy, 9
Water, 22, 76
Winged Monster, 10
Yei' bichei, 12
Yellow Corn Girl, 9

Daw, Curtie E., 18
Desolations Flats, 13
Dolores River, 67
Dominguez, 55

El Capitan, 78
Escalante, 55
Etcitty, Alex, 11, 13

family life
    ceremonies, 17
    children, 9, 20
    clanships, 20
    cradleboard, 20
    family love, 13
    food, 17
    matriarchy, 20
    purpose in life, 9
    sharing stories, 17
fancy dancer, 21
Farmington, 22

First Ruin, back cover
Four Corners region, 17, 18, 76
Frémont Peak, 50

Gallup, 43
Glen Canyon, 57
Glen Canyon Dam, 56
Goods of Value Mountain, 10
Grand Canyon, 60-61
Grand Staircase-Escalante NM, 55
Grants, New Mexico, 43
Grey Streak Mountain, 10

Hatathli (ritual singers) 18
hogan, 22-23, 46-48, 69
Holy Hogan, 23
Hopi, 50
Horseshoe Bend, 56
hosteen, 13
hozho, 13
Hualapai, 50
Huerfano Mesa, 10, 22, 76
Hunt's Mesa, front cover, 74-75
Hupa, 18

Kaibito Plateau, 17, 52
Karok, 18
Kicking off Rocks, 23

La Plata Range, 21, 67
Lake Powell, 7, 55, 57
Long Walk, 10, 20, 52
    Barboncito, 11, 12
    Bosque Redondo, 11, 20
    Carleton, James (Gen.) 10, 11
    Carson, Kit (Col.) 20
    Fort Sumner, 20
    Jackson, Andrew (Pres.) 11, 12
    Sherman, William Tecumseh (Gen.) 11, 12
    Turquoise Mountain, 12, 42
Lukachukai, 10
Lukachukai Mountains, 32

Mittens, 70-71
Monument Valley, 8, 25, 68-72, 74-75, 78
Mount Blanca (White Mountain) 20-21, 26-27
Mount Hesperus (Jet Mountain) 21, 66-67
Mount Sinai, 10
Mount Taylor (Turquoise Mountain) 9, 12, 22

Navajo
    Code Talkers, 43
    context of time, 16

Genesis, 10, 12
Holy Land, 10
    Mountain, 17
    photographer, 10, 12
    reservation, 17
    student, 13
    Tribal Fair, 13
Nazlini, 34
Newcomb, New Mexico, 40-41

Page (town) 7, 56, 58
Pecos River, 11
Pedernale Peak, 22
Pollen Mountain, 45
pow wow, 21
Puebloan (ancient), 38, 42

Red Mesa, 76-66
Rio Grande, 12, 67
Rock Mesa, 13
Rocks That Rush Together, 23

Salahkai Mesa, 35, 45
San Francisco Peaks (Abalone Shell Mountain) 21, 50-51
San Juan Mountains, 67
San Juan River, 23, 67
San Luis Valley, 27
Sangre de Cristo Range, 27
Sarsi, 18
Sekani, 18
Shiprock, 10, 23, 36
Spider Rock, 32
silversmithing, 18, 19
slot canyons, 20, 64-65
snakes, 19
Spaniards, 19
spirit line, 19

Taos Mountains, 23
Taylor, Zachary (Gen.) 43
Tunicha Range, 10
turquoise, 9, 19, 21, 79

Ventana Ridges, 29
Vermilion Cliffs, 63

Water Holes Canyon, 58
weaving, 18, 19
White Mesa and Arch, 52

Yavapai, 50
Yazzie, Christy, 2
Yei Bichei formation, 9
Yei'bichei chant, 12

Zuni, 50